# A Dose of Love

## English Quotes

VIBHA JAIN

NOTION PRESS

# NOTION PRESS

India. Singapore. Malaysia.

ISBN xxx-x-xxxxx-xx-x

*To some known and unknown people for appreciating my writings.*

Smile and shine, as both are free just
like our sun.

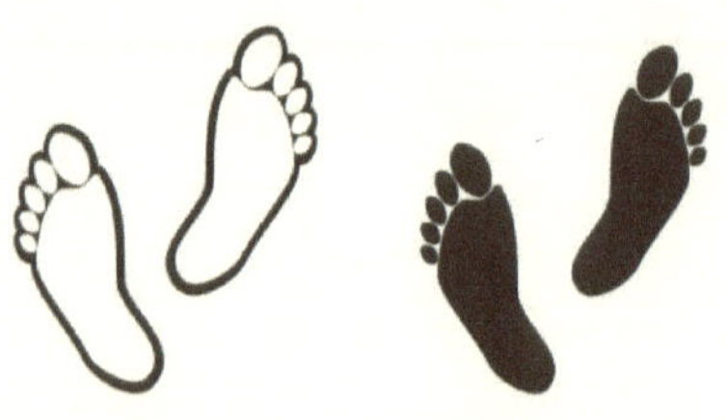

Don't take tension,

Send your tension on a vacation.

Early morning rains are like soothing
alarm music to the ears.

People will choose

different colours for you,

But always choose

your own favourite colour.

'Like' button on your post says:

Like your post first,

Love yourself first.

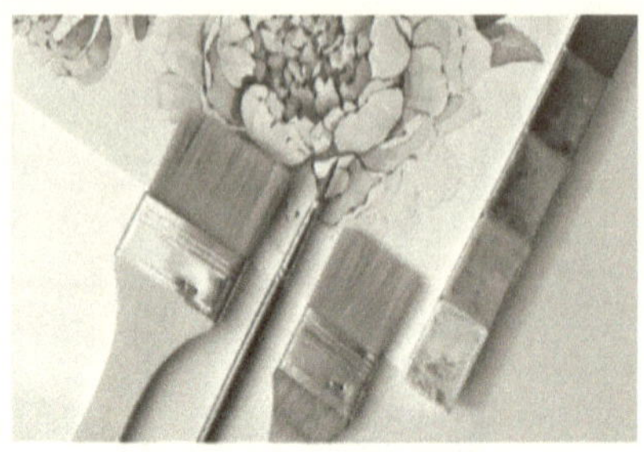

Art sometimes helps to

run away from the real

world for a moment

and get lost in the world of

colour, brushes, canvas,

paints and imagination.

Loneliness tastes like spending

time with God,

You feel no one's presence

physically,

But you can feel God's presence,

mentally.

Never miss a chance to
genuinely appreciate people.
It will make their day, and you
will also feel good.

Always appreciate your small achievements, because if you don't appreciate the smaller ones, you will not achieve the bigger ones.

If you can't become someone's rose, then please don't become someone's thorn.

Give your dose of love and care to only those people who truly deserve it.

The peacock is dancing in the rain.
Let's face the obstacles and start the
new game of life again.

An autumn leaf is a perfect example of how to see that change happens and nothing remains permanent in life.

Bad people sometimes give us those lessons which are impossible to learn from good people.

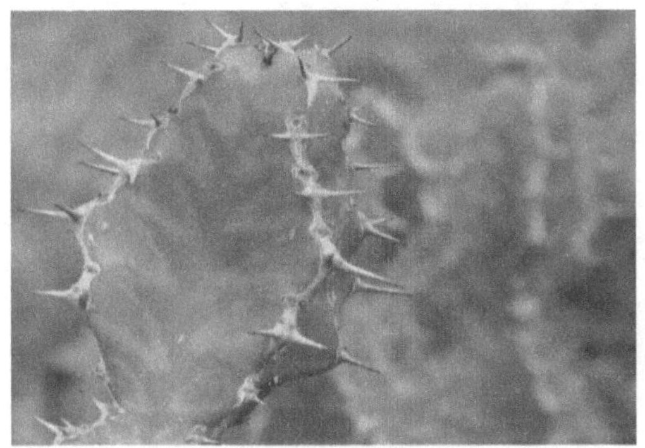

Be like a cactus and not like a flower, because people easily pluck flowers, but no one dares even touch the cactus.

Rain, Books and Hot Tea are a wonderful combination for reading and nature lovers.

"Truth" is like fruits and vegetables, which are healthy

&

"Lie" is like junk food, which is unhealthy.

Walking alone is better than walking with people who you know will backstab you for their own benefits.

Those people are blessings in your life who are good listeners and care to hear your whole conversation.

Little doses of jealousy are fine. But an overdose of jealousy proves to be poisonous.

It is better to run away from negative
people for your well-being.

Everyone is different, and you cannot force anyone to be like you.

Sometimes people need only one call
to mend the broken relations.

Carefully accept other's love, as some people don't know the difference between like and love.

Use your words

carefully, as words

also reflect your character.

Sometimes you stuck in those places

where you don't belong.

Feelings can change if you take someone's love for granted.

Toxic people are injurious to our mental health. Be alert and try to identify these people in your life. They can be anyone, even your closest ones as well.

In every relation, there are ups and downs, but if the relation has only downs, then that relation is not good for you.

It's only after growing up I realised
that playing with emotions and
feelings is also a game which some
people just love to play

One of the greatest lessons I have learned in life is to stay away from narcissistic people as much as possible.

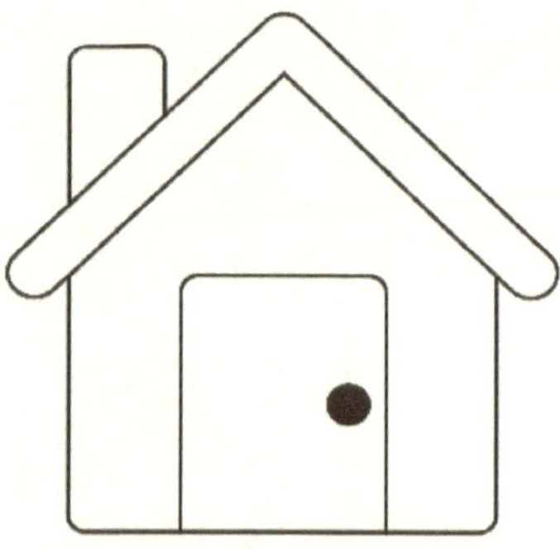

Having no regrets is like running down after knocking on someone's door.

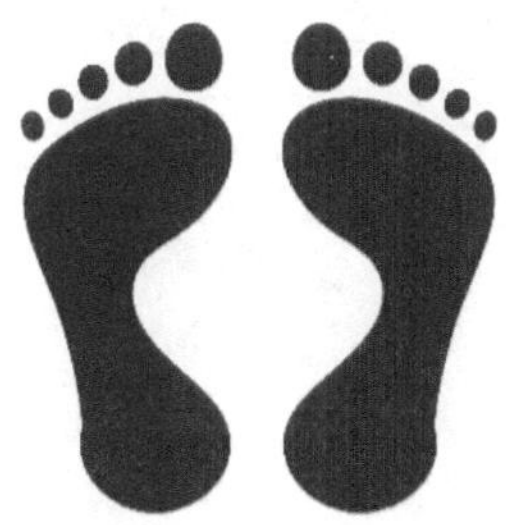

Getting out of the comfort zone is
like crossing a thorny path
barefooted to reach the goal.

Loving someone who doesn't love me back is like slapping myself with my hands.

Two things I never regret doing are taking a stand for myself and staying away from negative people.

Reading books is one of the best
stress busters.

Simplicity is that flower which is
original, not artificial.

The most difficult thing in life is to live with those people who don't love you.

Grief is that relative who irritates us so much that sometimes we start crying.

Love is that taxi ride that you take to reach your destination but then get stuck in the middle of traffic.

Hold your heart properly as occasionally it flies in the wrong direction.

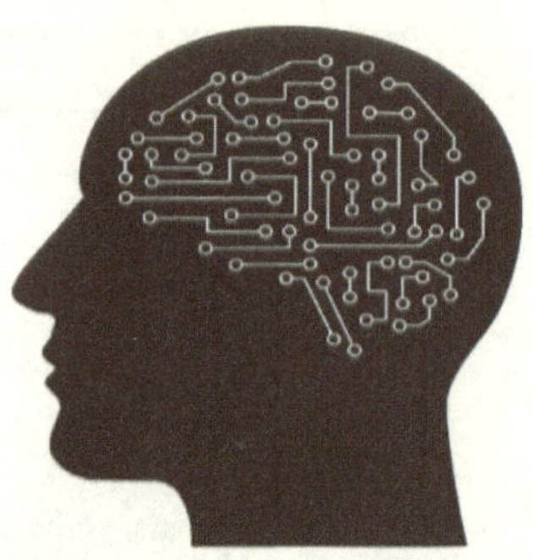

Try to grow beautiful and positive

thoughts in your mind.

Your pain will soon end just like an autumn leaf, and happiness will come just like a new leaf.

Never lose your self-confidence
because there are many good things
inside you.

Victory is when you defeat the
demons who reside in your mind.

Love, Hatred, Anger, Happiness, Sadness, Fear, Courage, Sympathy, Guilt, Jealousy are like the different colours of emotions. Different people choose and like different colours. It is up to us to choose which colours to use to create our own unique rainbow of emotions.

You have a beautiful soul,

take care of it.

Vibha is an Indian writer who originally belongs to Delhi, India. She has done B.Com. from Jabalpur, Madhya Pradesh, and a Diploma in Interior Designing from Kolkata, West Bengal. She also worked for a few months at an architectural firm in Delhi. She likes doing creative work and believes that writing also needs creativity. Apart from writing, she also loves reading, art, crafts, and photography.